For Jill —

Warm wishes

July 2010

DEDICATION

A wise lady once said "There is no hereditary aristocracy, decent people are the only true aristocrats."

In this age of extremism, we dedicate this collection to those 'true aristocrats' - ordinary decent human beings who have refused to buy into or be cowed by the populist in-vogue politics of race, religion and sectarianism.

It is specially for: zainah anwar, paddy maguiness, raja aziz addruse, kai nielsen, ahmad chik, rommel josef, eddin khoo, m. puravalen, ismail hashim, james lochead, malik imtiaz, haris fathillah, lim kean chye, jahaberdeen yunos, shuen lim, paul beasley, rohanna ariffin, arumugam palan, abdul rahim, lee kim siang, eric & jessica huntley and, most especially, to the indelible memory of my late lamented comrades-in arms, the great South African poet Dennis Brutus and the equally magnificent troubadour Adrian Mitchell.

Published by:
Bogle-L'Ouverture Press
P.O. Box 2186
London W13 9QZ
England

ISBN No. 0-904-52161-3

Cover Design by:
Leah T. Nash

Printed by:
Phoenix Printers Sdn. Bhd.
Penang, Malaysia.

Parables Prophets & Pillocks

Cecil Rajendra

BOGLE L'OUVERTURE PRESS

Contents

Testament I

Testament II

Contents

Contents

Testament IV

God, grant me the serenity
to accept the things i cannot change,
the courage to change the things i can
and the wisdom to know the difference.

- *Reinhold Niebuhr*

Human stupidity
is a bottomless abyss
and the ocean
i see from my window
seems to me
quite small by comparison.

- Gustave Flaubert -

Testament I

The earth also was corrupt before God;
and the earth was filled with violence.

Genesis VI verse 11

Wisdom is better than weapons of war:
but one sinner destroyeth much good.

Ecclesiastes IX verse 18

Impolitic Poetry

Politics in a literary work is a pistol shot in the middle of a concert, a crude affair though one impossible to ignore.

- Stendhal -

i have never
fingered a gun
in my life .....

so where do
they come from –
these pistol shots
in mid-reverie?

splattering egg
white folios
with blue/
black squiggles.

shattering canons
of cosy poesy;
exploding complacency!

Psalm 3

(After Mahmoud Darwish)

The day my poems
were of the earth
i became a companero of corn

The day my poems
were forged in anger
i became a confidant of chains

The day my poems
were hewed from rocks
i was made sweetheart of streams

The day my poems
were coined in revolt
i became the idol of earthquakes

but the day my poems
        dripped honey
flies began settling on my lips.

Unholy Legacy

"We will pass along to our children all the freedoms we enjoy – and chief among them is the freedom from fear."

- George W Bush -

In his State of the Union
address, the President
of the most powerful
nation promises future
generations assorted freedoms.

The President highlights
"freedom from fear";
stays silent on other
special freedoms he has
enjoyed during his tenure:

the freedom to pollute
& desecrate the environment;
the freedom to amass
weapons of mass destruction;

the freedom to bully
lie, invade & imprison;
the freedom to torture
& murder the innocent .....

Mr. President, are these too
some of the freedoms
you intend to
pass along to your children?

Shooting for Fun

"Actually it's fun to fight 'em, you know. It's a hell of a hoot. It's fun to shoot some people. I'll be right up front with you, I like brawling."

- Lt-Gen. James Mattis
Senior US Marine Corps General
Troop Commander in Iraq & Afghanistan

We're shooting 'em
        in Iraq
We're shooting 'em
        in Af-
ghan-i-stan .....
        Soon, we'll
be shooting 'em
        up
in North Korea
        then
moving down to Iran .....

After we've done Korea
        We'll
be shooting 'em in Libya
be shooting 'em in Syria
        perhaps
even over in Pakistan .....

I'll be right up front with you
        It's hell of a hoot
        It's fun to shoot
        Join us Marines
So you can shoot some people too.

Business As Usual In Burma

CHEVRON/TOTAL
PETRONAS/HALLIBURTON
What do they have in common?

Profits/Pipelines/Petroleum
Low Investment/High Dividends
Sealed with a kiss
& a kickback from the Junta.

WASHINGTON/PARIS
KUALA LUMPUR/LONDON
What do they spout in common?

Words of commiseration
for Aung San Su Kyi
A call for the return
of Myanmar to Democracy.

CHEVRON/TOTAL/PETRONAS/HALLIBURTON
WASHINGTON/PARIS/KUALA LUMPUR/LONDON
What do they do in common?

Business as usual with a bull-necked general
oiled with the sweat & blood of a side-lined people.

Unholy Terror

The 'DEMOCRACY! DEMOCRACY!' mantra
chokes under a blanket of smoke & gunfire.
Yesterday's euphoria
gives way
to static fear;
as green-
helmeted hoods of
the junta
mushroom everywhere
round temple & pagoda.

Streets, where monks marched
nine-abreast, to the ecstatic cheer
of demonstrators, stand deferential
once more, to the martial menace
of teargas, baton, bayonet & rifle.

In monasteries upcountry
- debouched of votaries -
the blood-splattered stupas
squat & wait in stony silence.

When a bruised, bloated burgundy-
robed corpse surfaces belly-
up in the muddy Irrawaddy
the juggernaut junta announce:
"Our country has returned to normalcy."

Confirming the Generals' metamorphosis
of Orwell's old Burma
into a new synonym for unholy Terror!

Guilty As Hell?

"If you harbour a terrorist; if you support a terrorist, if you feed a terrorist, you will be as guilty as the terrorist."

- President George Bush -

Not, of course
if you are one of us.....

If you are FBI
CIA or US Army
you can blow up
hotels & planes
detonate lives
with impunity.

Even
a convicted felon
involved in
the assassination
of a former
US of A President
can be eased
out of prison
by our CIA
& granted a pardon
by our White House;
but only, of course
if you are one of us.

But don't take
our word for it;
ask Luis
Clemente Posada –
ex-CIA, FBI
US Army officer;
ex-Havana
hotel, Cubana
jetliner bomber;
ex-prisoner
& our very own home-
trained mass murderer.

Imprisoned in Venezuela
for killing seventy-three;
sprung by our Agency
now enjoying the good life
incognito somewhere in Miami!

Even The Grass .....

One evening, after the Sun
had dropped into that bowl
of blood – we call the Sea –
splashing the sky with fire.

i found myself in our garden
muttering to our flowers;
mumbling the insanity
of war, the pain, the terror .....

in the middle of a tale
about a mother losing her
only child in the cross-fire,
i heard something softly rustle;

glancing across my shoulder
i caught blades of grass –
newly shorn that morning –
beginning to hackle in horror.

Clusters

While a cluster
of culprits
most guilty
of using
manufacturing
profiting
from cluster bombs
vacillate
over that Treaty ......

Clusters
of curious children
frolicking
in the orange
groves of Lebanon
have their limbs
ripped off daily.

The Price of Innocence

PATHA (INDIA): A butcher in eastern India killed the 8-year-old son of a customer who owed him 20 rupees (US 50cents). He pushed the boy into a well after the child's father failed to pay for meat bought the previous month.

- AP -

He was so small
        always marginal;
news of his murder
        barely made a filler
in the foreign news
column of the Times.

In the ledger
of that butcher
his life was worth
less than 50-cents.

Yet, the evening
of his drowning
saw a million
angry asterisks
****
splash the nightsky;
pulsing expletives
hurled by angels
outraged at the waste
of another innocent.

Coming Full Circle

A ruling Party leader
whose racist remark
raised racial tension
throughout the nation ...
was given a wrist-slap
& a nominal suspension.

The newspaper reporter
whose innocent act
was reporting the fact
of his racist remark
was detained under
the Internal Security Act.

A concerned lady citizen
remarking that the treatment
smacked of "double standards"
is now subject of a complaint:
"her remarks are seditious
& aimed at creating racial tension."

She is now under police investigation.
Note: in our beloved Nation
There is neither
Political nor gender discrimination.

A Threat to National Security

She was taken into detention
the Home Minister explained:
"as her life was under threat."

She was released from detention
the Police Inspector said:
"as she was no threat to Security."

Which raises another question:
Did the threat to the life
of the reporter detained under
the Internal Security Act
pose a threat to national security?

Rats!

(for christopher leong, wee choo keong, robert lazar, ranjit singh, m puravalen, razlan hadin & yeo yang poh)

There are rats everywhere
not only in drains & sewers
but also in Cabinets & chambers.

Busy burrowing hither
& thither, sowing a virus
more contagious than typhus.
Not our common rodent *Rattus*
rattus, but its human
equivalent - homo contemptus.

These vermin paralysed an
entire nation with a plague
not bubonic, but endemic, corruption.

In Asia in the 21st Century
as in Europe in the 14th Century
a right Royal Commission
of rat-catchers was cobbled
to summon & root out rats
responsible for this contagion.

As the Bar & Bench rats
in sleek black coats
pattered in one by one
with a litany of denials:

> "It may look like me ...
> It may sound like me ...
> But I'm not certain it's me."

The acrid smell
of rodent seared our nostrils.

Now in the advent
of the Chinese
lunar Year of the Rat
a nation holds its breath ...
Will the plague be
arrested in the year of the rodent?

Lost in Transition

From overhead squeaking, ceiling
fans to central air-conditioning;

From Remington typewriters
to Microsoft computers;

From bulky, black, bakelite
phones to blackberry & website;

From urbane lay-magistrates
to green, wet-eared graduates;

From public defender J.R. Logan
to wheeler-dealer V.K. Lingam;

Somewhere in the transition
of our judicial system
from colonial to modern
Corruption
        has crept in .....
& Justice
        like those swiftlets
that once inhabited
eaves of the old courthouse
        has taken wing .....

Political Stunts & Stents

(for Hor Lin)

The question is not
whether medical stents
          - bare metal
            drug-coated
            or, plastic -
help heart patients
with clogged arteries
live richer, fuller lives.

The real question is
is there a stent
          - gingko-coated
            bamboo
            or, otherwise –
we can insert
into the brains
of our politicians
to help unclog
the thinking
of these blockheads!

Mud-Skippers

"Mudskippers are drawn to muddy ecosystems. In some countries, mudskippers are used as a pollution indicator."

- Dr. Aileen Kan Shau Hwai -
Universiti Sains Malaysia

With oversize head
myopic pop-out
foraging eyes
and versatile flippers...
these shrimp-like
slippery, slimy creatures
skip nonchalant
from this bank
to that, then back ...
prompted only by
an appetite & the tide ...

Anthropologists
far and wide
come see them
perform their
self-serving antics ...
not in mangrove swamp
but in the mud and murky
waters of our politics!

Boson & Morons: God's Particles

From the atom
came the proton
and the neutron

From an election
came the Pakatan
and the Barisan

From neutron & proton
we got the quark & gluon

From the Barisan & Pakatan
we got some quare politicians

Now to find the smallest
particle – 'the Higgs boson' –
believed to give mass
to all other particles
scientists built the biggest
collider somewhere near Geneva

No such trouble attends
discovering the smallest mind
in all of God's kingdom .....
they can always be found
in imbeciles in collision
in the corridors of Parliament.

Rocket-scientist MPs

The powers
of deduction
of our
Parliamentarians
is often
beyond ken
or comprehension.

Take their
latest
proposition
in the august
House
that HIV
victims
deliberately
choose
their infection.

In the same
fashion
(i wonder)
that
Honourable
Members
choose
to be infected
by the virus
of idiocy
after Election?

Buy-election

PAS spiritual leader Nik Abdul Aziz Nik Mat posted in his blog that a vote for party PAS (whose symbol is the moon) is a vote for Islam and happiness in the hereafter. Whereas, a vote for party UMNO (whose symbol is the kris) is a vote for corruption as its by-election candidate was found guilty of money politics by his own party.

If
a vote
for
the Kris
is
a vote
for corruption

Is
a vote
for
the Moon
a pass-
port
to heaven?

Polar Bears Don't Lie

Polar bears don't lie
Politicians do ....
Penguins can't fly
will surely die
It's up to me, up to you.

Flame & famine
Flood & fire
there's no denying
we are melting ....
2 degrees over
& we all go under
What to do? What to do?

Polar bears don't lie
Politicians do ....
Penguins can't fly
will surely die
It's up to me, up to you.

Over a round table
our leaders haggle
over cuts & costs ....
but for a dollar
will pimp our future
to the highest bidder
What to do? What to do?

Polar bears don't lie
Politicians do ....
Penguins can't fly
will surely die
It's up to me, up to you.

When rich nations
from poor relations
can buy permits
to release green-
house gasses ....
we're all screwed!
What to do? What to do?

Polar bears don't lie
        Politicians do ....
Penguins can't fly
        will surely die
It's up to me, up to you.

Where political resolutions
like carbon emissions
remain little more than
puffs of hot air -
smog pies in the sky ....
you can breathe your last sigh
What to do? What to do?

Polar bears don't lie
        Politicians do ....
Penguins can't fly
        will surely die
It's up to me, up to you.

Thou shalt not raise a false report
put not thine hand with the wicked
to be an unrighteous witness.

Exodus XXIII verse 1

These six things doth the Lord hate:
yea, seven are an abomination unto him:
a proud look, a lying tongue and hands that shed innocent blood, a heart that deviseth wicked imaginations, feet that be swift in running to mischief, a false witness that speaketh lies and him that soweth discord among brethren.

Proverbs VI verses 16-19

Testament II

Organised Crime & Religion

All religions claim
divine guidance
in their tenets
of peace & tolerance.

Yet, no week passes
when someone is not
shot, blown to pieces
in the name of God.

So, who's to blame?

The Supreme Being
who looks down
on us with benevolence .....

Or, those Godfathers
who organize
factions in His name?

A Different Sameness

Each one different
yet akin.....
under our tent
of skin
our bones are white
our blood is red
& when dead
all flesh, as a poet
once said,
is food for the maggot.

Race, opinion, religion .....
little
more than brushstrokes
on
a galactic canvas.
Yet
rather than celebrate
our
diverse variegations
(as one often rejoices
in the colours of Spring
Sunset, Flowers, the Rainbow)
We
choose to exterminate
blow
each other up over
less than
minor shades of difference.

Not Thunder

Not thunder
nor any
alien power .....
only that lightning rod
of race/religion
greed/corruption
can split
          this God-
given green
& lovely land asunder.

If Only Our Prophets Were Women
(for Zainah Anwar & SIS)

If only our Prophets were Women
the History of our World
would have been so very different.

Abraham, Moses
Muhammad, Jesus –
good men, all of them
who preached Peace
Love & Universal Brotherhood.
But MEN, nonetheless .....

Still, it must be admitted
(Message of Love, aside)
men who boldly flaunted
a strong feminine side
in choice of kaftan & coiffure .....
Not by chance opting in favour
of soft sandals over jackboots;
billowing ankle-length dresses
over armour suits & khaki shorts;
& long flowing tresses over crewcuts.

Yet, despite their best intentions
our prophets' entire experience
of the Milk of Human Goodness
was culled wholly from infancy;
unlike their mothers & sisters
none of them suckled a baby;
all, ALL, were Takers not givers.

Likewise, their ungiving followers
 - men, for the most part –
who chose to ignore the soft
warm message of the heart
& focus more on the hard
macho precepts of their Masters.

Abdicating Love for the Sword
to spread the Word of God;
preferring summary execution
(of enemy, infidel & Saracen)
to gentle persuasion
& the art of subtle seduction.

If only our prophets were women
consider how the history/herstory
of war would have been written ...

Instead of being fought
years on end in trenches,
the First World War
would have been slugged
to a standstill in minutes
between a broad Scottish lass
& a buxom Bavarian fraulein
in a mud-wrestling rink
somewhere on the Maginot Line.

In the Second World War,
would we ever have found
a woman willing to dump
that atom bomb on Hiroshima?
And not only because of their
legendary fear of flying,
but can anyone sane imagine
any lady, dropping from height,
A-Baby nicknamed 'Little Boy'?

Women would have converted
the Crusades to Masquerades
(complete with funny hats
  silver-masks & sequins);
the Seven Years' War
into a seven-year-itch.
The Battle of the Bulge
into a Battle of Boobs
& resolved the War of Roses
          ...with roses!

Can anyone sober picture
even for a single second:
Mary Magdalene hoisting a rifle?
Ibu Fatimah with an AK-47?
or, Mother Theresa with a bazooka?

If only our prophets were women
the Herstory of our World
would have been so different .....
for starters, we would have been
bequeathed Universal Motherhood
not bloody Brotherhood or Martyrhood.

If only ALL our Prophets were Women

Singing Not Praying

(for the singing clans of Ireland – the Sands,
the Rooneys, The Corrs, the Maguinesses etc. etc.)

"The family
        that
 prays together
 stays together ….."

Their parents
        often
preached at
the dinner table.

Not long after
these same parents
        Divorced;
splitting the family
in four directions.

Mother & Father
leaving to pursue
their separate careers;
        dumping
4 shell-shocked children
with their grandparents.

Perhaps a better
option to prayer
to glue a family
        Together
would be a song
sung in harmony.

Fast & Feasting

Greed & Consumption
have subverted
this holy month
of fasting & abstinence
into an extended
binge of feasting
& unholy indulgence.

Every hotel, restaurant
café & coffee-house
has been fast
to cash in on
our season of Ramadan.

Pull-outs, Supplements
flyers & full-page
colour advertisements
unabashed offer:
'A Fiesta of Food'
'Feasts for the Fasting Month'.

'Break your fast
in Style', beckons
one 5-Star Hotel
trumpeting more
than 300 varieties
of Malay cuisine;
with a selection
of Ghazal songs
& 'tasteful' dances
to tantalize your spleen.

Yet another invites
one to 'break your
fast with traditional
balik kampung dishes
that *nenek* (grandma)
used to make
in the good old days.'

For 'only' 100 ringgit
plus plus per person
You can savour
Ikan Tongkol Percik
Udang Galah Cili Padi
Daging Lemak Cili Api
Burung Puyuh Berempah
Kerabu Nangka Muda
et cetera, et cetera, et cetera.

Then, to further
'tempt your tastebuds'
you can stop by their
Japanese & Western stations
each crammed tight
with a crowd of delights:
like Sushi & Sashimi
Salmon in Puff Pastry
Oyster Rockefeller
& Spicy Chicken Shawarma.

i well remember
the good old days
in our fishing village
of Tanjong Tokong
where my football
mate's grandmother
(whom all of us
addressed as 'nenek')
fed her entire
family on less
than one hundred
ringgit per month;
& every Ramadan
broke her humble fast
not with exotic dates
(as our dowager Datins)
but a simple prayer, a glass
of tap water & a dry biscuit.

Whither Our Constitution?

In this land
        of freedom
moderation, tolerance .....

Our 'moral'
        guardians
first arrived
        with torches
to reduce
        a god-
fearing commune
        to ashes.

When structures
        'deviant'
failed to crackle
        the 'moral'
mob brought in
        their bulldozers.
The village is now
a heap of rubble.

It mattered not a jot
all violence
emanated from without;
It mattered not a jot
all those cowed within -
men, women & children -
offered no resistance .....

The victims were herded
carted off to prison;
the perpetrators praised
as heroes of their religion!

Death Throes
(for Haris & Jabbar)

In the remains
of an evening .....
as we sit
in Sunset Café
(with our Sun-
day newspapers)
watching
the horizon
rise to squash
& swallow whole
an over-ripe
Sunkist sun;
then betel-spit
her life-juice
& bloody pips
against a sullen sky .....

my mind turns
East to flames
in Sky Kingdom;
a giant tea-pot
a giant umbrella
a quiet commune
& a red-faced
mob carrying
a giant coffin
hell-bent
on burying
all remnants
of religious freedom!

Do Not Be Misled

National Fatwa Council
Chairman warned people
not to seek knowledge
from political ulama:

"Muslim teachers
with political
agendas spawn
fanatical scholars."

"Ulama should not
use their personal
interest in politics
to woo the people."

He made these remarks
after presenting a talk
on the Prime Minister's
thinking on Islam .....

The PM, the Chair said
was a shining example
of a rational scholar
who was a-political!

God-forsaken Religions

Any religion
that sidelines
excludes
          any one.

Any religion
that does not
open doors to
          every one.

Any religion
that claims
it's "the one
and only one".

Any religion
whose language
is "we" / "they"
and not "us".

All such religions
run against God
who is Oneness
& abhors divisions.

Serving God

Sick of the terror
fear & confusion
visited each day
on his constituents
from those threats
        (in the Bible)
of death & destruction
by flood & famine
& locust infestation ....

US Senator Ernie
sought to protect
"millions & millions
of the Earth's people
from terrorization"
with a permanent
        INJUNCTION
against the Almighty.

The Senator's application
was first accepted
then rejected by the Registry
on realization
that the Court process server
would be unable
to serve the Summons
at God's unlisted home address!

Peace That Passeth Understanding

JERUSALEM: Israeli police, with assault rifles, rushed to the Church of the Holy Sepulcher and arrested two clergymen after a brawl erupted next to the site of Jesus' tomb in Golgotha. A bearded Armenian monk in a red-and-pink robe and a black-clad Greek Orthodox monk with a bloody gash on his forehead were taken away in handcuffs.

- Associated Press -

Jesus died too soon. He would have repudiated his doctrine if he had lived to my age.

- Friedrich Nietzsche -

And who will argue
with the philosopher
who also proclaimed
the death of Yahweh?

Certainly not when
pious monks clash
to slash each other
over a right of way.

And riot policemen
in battle regalia
are summoned in
to quell the affray

keep bloody factions
apart & restore restive
peace at the Sepulcher
of our Prince of Peace .....

The Siege Mentality

Up North in Switzerland
right-wing populists
vote to ban minarets
as a threat to
Swiss architectural integrity.

Down South in Bolehland
Christian texts
containing the word 'Allah'
are confiscated
as a threat to National Security.

Right-wing Swiss populists
Self-righteous Islamists
wardens of national identity
defenders of religious purity
both espousing artistic
freedom & religious tolerance.

But can anyone tell the Difference?

Mantra & Fatwa

The Mantra:
Malaysia, truly Asia! –
a moderate, democratic
progressive Muslim nation
heedful of all its children.

The Fatwa:
Breakdancing & Rock music
are haram & forbidden
they are the tools of Satan.

The Mantra:
Malaysia, truly Asia! –
a modern, gender-bias-
free, liberal democracy
respectful of all women.

The Fatwa:
sporting short hair & trousers
is a no-no for Ninnie
as it might turn her lesbian.

The Mantra:
Malaysia, truly Asia! –
a multi-racial, forward-
looking, Islamic nation
mindful of all religions.

The Fatwa:
the ancient practice of Yoga
is henceforth banned, Verboten!
practitioners might turn deviant.

Malaysia, truly, truly Asia?

Horror Tales - Real & Fictional

So many horror
stories we hear:

of women lashed
for drinking a beer
of women gouged
for eyeing a neighbour

of women caged
for driving a vehicle
of women raped
for showing an ankle

of women whipped
for wearing a bra
of women flogged
for not wearing a burka

So many horror
stories we hear
through newspaper
internet & television

Yet, the women's
division of our largest
political party
passes a resolution

<u>not</u> against real
hour-upon-hour
everyday horror
visited upon women

but the fictional
unreal horror films
we see on cinema-
screen & television;

for fictional, not real
horror stories, they reckon
pose the greater threat
towards corrupting religion!

Nietzsche, God & Me ...

he could not believe
        i believed
in a Supreme Being.

I always took you
for an atheist, he said.

unless some atheist
        can prove
God does <u>not</u> exist
        i shall
be a believer
        i said
though not a follower
        of any religion
dictated by dogmatists.

he remained skeptical
until i recalled
a lesson gleaned
from graffiti scrawled
in a London urinal:

NIETZSCHE SAID:
GOD IS DEAD!
GOD SAID:
NIETZSCHE IS DEAD!

Q.E.D.

21st Century Crusade

Our latter-day Crusader
unsheathes his sabre
raises it ....
"Let this serve as a warning
to anyone who challenges our race
to anyone who questions our religion."

Our latter-day Crusader
kisses his sabre
brandishes it ....
"Do not play with fire
our warrior blood is heated
we will fight you to the end."

But fellow citizens, never fear
We are not racists or extremists
For the fist is a symbol of peace
And the sword a symbol of justice.

Our latter-day Crusader
waves his sabre
his fellow warriors roar:
"When will you use it?
We are willing to bathe in blood
in defence of our race & religion."

But fellow citizens, never fear
We are not racists or extremists
For the fist is a symbol of peace
And the sword a symbol of justice.

Kill To Stop Killing

Invoking
the fourth commandment:
THOU SHALT NOT KILL ....

Espousing the sanctity of life
before birth, bible-
quoting, God-fearing
regular church-going
pro-life anti-
abortionist Scott Roeder ....

Strolled
into the house of God
one Sunday morning
said a short prayer
drew his revolver
shot & killed abortion-
doctor George Tiller.

Here endeth
the first lesson
on how to kill
to stop the killing ....

God-fearing Men

In his memoirs, "Decisions: My Life in Politics", former German Chancellor Gerhard Schroeder said he could not reconcile himself with the feeling that religion was the driving force behind many of President Bush's political decisions. "What bothered me, and in a certain way made me suspicious, was how much this President, again and again, described himself as God-fearing."

- A.P. -

War-mongering
Presidents
suicide bombers
pious arsonists
are never found
amid the ranks
of the Godless
atheist or agnostic.

But are ever
culled from
that congregation
of God-fearing
men who insist
they are neither
extremist nor fanatic.

Be afraid
be very afraid
of those God-fearing
men lurking in our midst!

The Misunderstood Fundamentalist

Grossly misunderstood
my religion is Love
Universal Brotherhood
Peace, Compassion
Goodness, Kindness
Patience, Tolerance
Forgiveness, Openness
without guile or guise ....

& I'll slit the throat
of anyone who holds otherwise!

Testament III

Set me as a seal upon thine heart,
as a seal upon thy arm;
for love is strong as death;
jealousy cruel as the grave:
the coals thereof are coals of fire
which hath a most vehement flame.

Song of Solomon VIII verse 6

Discovery Channel

That first time
is like no other ....

going down
down down
to a
sacred mound;

parting
the thicket
discovering
a rivulet
running
from a
hitherto un-
charted cavern.

Inching up
virgin territory;
up, up to
that barrier
before breaking
through
in a spectacular
explosion
of blood & ecstasy!

Auto-Pilot

In those wee
        hours
of a morning
        when
all our souls
        inhabit
that limbo
        'twixt
sleep & waking
        where
one's reflexes
        run
on automatic ....

I often catch
        my
left arm
        snaking
out to ensure
        your
soft warm body
        is
still there
        softly
breathing beside me.

Countdown

So many, many years
        have passed
in a whoosh ....
        though never
too many years.
        Together
we've grown so old;
        but
for the grace of God
        not yet
decrepit or alzheimic.

As, inexorable, we
        hurtle
towards the crematorium
        I sometimes
stop to conduct a one-
        man moratorium
on this marathon
        union
of over-the-top intensity.

The good, bad & so often
        mad times
our blood & passion-fuelled
        sessions ....
now, admittedly, somewhat
        sporadic;
yet never staid, perfunctory
        or missionary
but always, always breathless
        seismic!

And those impossible-to-predict
        insane
irrational explosions of anger
        where
across the kitchen floor
        volcanic
we've eyeballed each other
        with
shades of murderous intent.

Still, even in those taut
hours of bitterest rancour
there was .... no other;
& all that shouting & screaming
never once undermined the loving.

Small Everyday Things

Don't think
the everyday things
you do for me
like the ironing
the cooking
the internetting
the dropping-off
& the picking up
the once-in-three-
week haircut
your neat roll-up
of my fresh-
ly laundered socks
don't think
any of these things
have gone unnoticed.

Despite my nonchalance
my don't-give-a-fuck air
Somewhere in the ledger
of my heart, it's all there
          every thing
everything's been duly recorded.

Passion

If you have never
felt like strangling
with bare hands
the woman you love.

If you have never
felt like mowing down
the stranger flirting
with the woman you love.

If you have never
felt like slitting
open your wrists
over the woman you love.

You
have never loved.
Love & Death
ride the razor's edge.

Handkerchiefs
(after Mahmoud Darwish)

Like the marble
tombs of martyrs
is your silence
stretching, stretching
          interminable ....

Now i recall
how your hands
used to hover
over my heart
          like birdwings.

Do not worry
          my love
about the origins
of lightning .....
leave that
for the dusky
horizons to figure.
Steel your mind
instead for other
thoughts, thoughts
of bruised kisses
of days of drought
& death, my death
& all those sorrows
that attend mourning.

The handkerchiefs
we exchanged
on parting
are nothing
but shrouds billowing
in the wind
that blows in
          cinders
floods the village
with blood, tears
& a fierce yearning.

Return to me
          my love
those handkerchiefs
sighs of our parting,
for our longed-for
Reunion remains
a distant promise
growing ever growing
in this my exile.

And do not cry
          my love
at repeated deaths;
for i have nothing
left of you except
the memory of your eyes.

And never wear
those parting
handkerchiefs
as souvenirs
of love songs;
for i would rather
you wrap in them
        my love
the wounds
        of our homeland.

Falling in Lust

Why is it
in my dreams
of you
no violins
play in
the background
only flutes
& triangles ....

Why is it
no rolling hills
or meadows
compose
the landscape
i paint of you
in my mind's eye
only gaping craters
& belching volcanoes ....

Why is it
in our fantasies
you never
peel me a grape;
it is
always i
splitting a fig
or feeding you a banana ....

Why is it
the boudoirs
of my brain
are filled
not with roses

but arum lilies;
& the fragrance
is always musk
never lavender ....

could it be
that we
have fallen in lust?

Politically Incorrect Love Poem

People are beginning to talk
about our time together, Paddy.

Of our common passion
for music, song, poetry
of our insane vision
of a world without
injustice or poverty ....

People are beginning to talk, Paddy.

And Deborah's getting jealous
And Rebecca's mighty suspicious.

And it isn't just about
our meeting at a seminar
our drinking in the pub
or, our cooking in the kitchen.

It's something I cannot figure.
Do you think it's about our
deep, shared, sacred love
for oh-so-fragrant Coriander?

Yes, people are beginning to talk, Paddy.

Memo To A Poet In The North

Here
we have too much sun ....

Everywhere
across this island
orchards sweat & groan
under the weight of fruit:
mangoes, mangosteens
papayas, durians, jackfruit ....

Even in our garden
heavy & overladen
our solitary rambutan tree
has been bent over
like a spondolytic woman.

I have harvested
some of our sun's
fecund rays
for inclement times.

so, if words frostbitten
sometimes hang sterile
in the icy tundras of your mind ....

call me!
I shall send shards
of our tropic sun
to unfreeze & ripen your poems.

Still Beautiful

the semi-final decider
that sent Barcelona
into the Champions League
final with United
in Roma, spelled
another night of insomnia ....

A manic Manchester
supporter since the glory
days of the Busby Babes
– when that holy Trinity
of Charlton, Law & Best
held passion & magic
over spoiled-brat hysterics –
I never could enjoy dinner
or a good night's sleep
before any major MU fixture.

I well remember
the night they
booted me out of
London's Poetry Society
for suggesting Sir
Bobby and <u>not</u> Betjeman
Hughes or Larkin
was Britain's greatest
poet of the Sixties;
adding salt to injury
by insisting Bobby
packed more poetry
in his left boot
than all those other
scribblers put together!

But back to Roma
& that Final where
after all the inflated
humbug & hoopla
of United, the thread-
needle passes of Barca
unstitched their fancy
multi-million outfit
& deflated Sir Fergie
like the punctured
inner bladder of one
of those old lace-up
leather footballs of yore.

Strangely, this debacle
did not evoke the usual
post-defeat nausea
but somewhere
the heart enjoyed
a private chuckle
at the victory of poetry
passion & magic
over mega-bucks
hype & histrionics
in what still
remains a beautiful game.

The Symphony of Silence

Words grate ....
& taken singly
or,
in sentences
- without
the silence
in-between -
are bereft
of music
or meaning ....

So,
to arrive
at the essence
of a poem
listen
to its silence.

The song
& the symphony
lie in that silence.

Testament IV

But thou, O Lord, shalt laugh at them;
thou shalt have all the heathen in derision.

Psalm LIX verse 8

Even in laughter the heart is sorrowful;
and the end of that mirth is heaviness.

Proverbs XIV verse 13

Down But Up

While a financial
crisis tumbled markets
from New York to Tokyo ....

it was 'business-as-usual'
reported Madam X
of an Australian bordello.

"Sex, like tobacco,"
she said, "is the only
true blue-chip industry".

"Even during times
of an economic down-
turn, our customers'
needs remain bullish
and up. There is no
slump!" she concluded.

The Potent Pail

Kuala Terengganu, Malaysia. The Syariah High Court here granted permission to Abu Bakar Embong, who has three wives and 25 children, to take a fourth wife, 30 years his junior.

- The Star -

Syabas syariah!
Syabas Abu Bakar!
father of twenty-five
husband to three
on getting the go-
ahead to marry
wife number four.

On being asked if
he was confident
of fathering more
with his new bride,
superdad replied:
"I foresee no problem
the secret, you see
of staying sexually
strong in old age
is this: when you
take your early
morning bath ...
you must pour
a pail of water
first down your
right leg before
wetting any other
part of your body."

“This is a must
for all good Muslims
practising polygamy,”
added the granddad
hoping to raise
his tally of offspring
up to a magical thirty.

Hibiscus

(for askandar)

Some pink, some red
        petals soft
infolded, intricate
        aroma subtle
        flavour delicate
releasing attar only
        to gentle
press, caress & palpate ....

I sing in praise
of hibiscus incarnate
        national flower
        national treasure
blossoming unchecked
        wild or domestic
in garden, jungle, temple
        & 'twixt
the thighs of every Cik!

Wreath for St. Valentine

Rejecting
obvious first passes
Juliet smiles
shakes her tresses ....

No, she is not
willing to put out
on their first date.

Yet
the maid purses
her rosebud lips in
an invitational pout.

Misreading signals
Romeo, the lout
                    swoops
with rapier
tongue to
invade her moue.

Firm, still gentle
Juliet pushes
Romeo off her ....
flutters twin butter-
fly eyelids down
down at the lad's
fast thickening spout.

Enough already
of this romance
this messing about ....
in our 21st Century
an amorous lady's
lips oft cry out for
meatier sustenance!

E D Martyrs

Umar Farouk Abdulmuttalab - dubbed the 'underwear bomber' - attempted to blow up North West Airlines Flight 253 on Christmas Day 2009 with a bomb strapped to his genitals.

- Reuters -

Question for a theologian:

if a plane-full
of infidels
is blown up
by a would-be
martyr
with a bomb
in his underwear ....

how would he
(our martyr)
deflower
his 72 virgins
on arrival in heaven?

Why Don't They Treat Old Men With Reverence?

(for Lim Chuin Wei)

Why don't they treat
old men, these days
          with reverence?

Yesterday
we were honoured
with complimentary adjectives
like 'great', 'grand' & 'wise';
today, society
prefixes us with expletives
like 'grumpy', 'silly' & 'dirty'.

Yesterday
we were respected as 'elders'
put on a pedestal;
today we're ridiculed
as 'old age pensioners'
shunted into an
old folk's home or hospital ....

why don't they treat'
old men, these days
          with reverence?

in the old days
in old India
they revered us as 'Sadhus'
- sought our counsel.

Nowadays
in new Malaysia
they revile us as 'Goondus'
- a bunch of old fools!

In the old days
in old China
virile old men
were given ginseng
the thumbs-up
& presented with
a pretty young maiden.

These days, wherever
if we are still
able to get it up
we're called *'hum-sup'*
& carted off to prison!

why can't they treat
old men, these days
with reverence?

Old

you know
you've crossed
the threshold
    to 'old' ...

when carbuncles
sprout in
strange places
& strangers
call you 'uncle'

when the hair
in your ear
grows thicker
& faster than
the hair
on your pate.

when morning
finds joints
& digits
of your every
other limb
stiffer
than that one
jointless limb.

you know
you've crossed
the threshold
    to 'old'.

Perils of the Native Tongue

Already you've mastered
the colloquialisms
of our local bazaar ....

"Aiyoh!" you complain
"so difficult, man,
your lingua franca ....
easy enough to speak
but so hard to read, lah."

"Just when I learn
that teksi is taxi
and pos means post
they tell me
pas is not past
but a political party!"

"And is it only
to confuse us
silly foreigners
that gas is gas
but air spells water;
bus is bas
dead is mati
but a dead bus
is not basmati?"

"and pray tell me why
when the word for
butter is mentega
& fly is terbang
do natives titter
when I call a butter-
fly – mentega terbang?"

"aiyoh! so difficult, lah
learning your Malaysia Bahasa!"

Soap

Soap
<u>in</u> a box
cleanses
the body.

Soap
<u>on</u> the Box
fuzzes
the mind.

Skin clear ....
Brain blur ....
Soap!

Humbag

The front cover
of DELTA
Buyer's Guide
is emblazoned:
"SAY NO
TO PLASTIC BAGS!"

The back page continues:
'Thinking of living green?
Join & support us ....
We can lessen
our footprints
by minimizing
use of plastic bags.
Just one simple action
is needed. Shop at
Delta without carrying
a plastic bag away!
Help us in the role
by saying "NO" today!'

Just one simple problem:
DELTA Buyer's Guide
arrives at my doorstep
in a see-thru' plastic bag!

The Egg

(for Deborah)

An egg is an egg
but a boiled egg
is a perfect creature.

A gleaming white
oval of un-
surpassed symmetry
encasing a flawless
sphere of yellow.

Some folks say:
an egg is also
a perfect metaphor.

Like a half-boiled
Englishman
justifying China's
annexation
of Tibet, for instance.

But polemics are
of little consequence
& Mathematics
cannot
resolve any argument.

Only this, I know
I shall never
write a poem
as perfect as an egg.

Pickles & Poems

Making a poem
is no different
from making a pickle.

There can be no
compromise
in its composition.

The theme:
love/death
mango/lime
(once chosen)
you proceed
to select
the choicest
words/spices
to bind
your concoction.

Verbs, vowels
syllables ....
ginger, garlic
chili, tumeric
cumin, cardamom
fenugreek
& mustard seed ....
each ingredient set
in precise proportion.

And do not forget
the oil & vinegar
the silence/hiatus
that separates
& holds
the whole together.

Then, a step back
to allow
the mixture
marinate
at its own pace
in our broiling sun.

For, one cannot
tell for sure
when a pickle/poem
is mature -
has found its level;
the proof is
all in the tasting.

A perfect poem
like a perfect pickle
will burst like a
flamenco on one's tongue.

The Pugilistic Poetry Prize

Stung by the New Yorker dubbing James Fenton, the Oxford Professor of Poetry, as 'Auden's Heir', poet Adrian Mitchell issued the following challenge: "You may be the professor but here comes the messer; see you in the ring."

Ladies and Gentlemen
Welcome to Wembley
to the first Poetry
Title Fight in Gt. Britain.

In the right corner
wearing blue shorts
is James 'The Perfesser'
Fenton from Oxon.

And in the left corner
sporting red trunks
is Adrian 'The Messer'
Mitchell from London.

Roundelaly One and Adrian
charges **Out Loud** from his corner
launching his **Oxford Hysteria**
at the trochee of his opponent.

Though aptly accoutred
in his florid **Kingfisher**
Boxing Gloves, 'The Perfesser'
is caught and winded.

He adopts a defensive stanza;
blocks a pantun combination
resuscitates his Asian connection
and counters with a tanka.

Thrown off rhythm, Adrian
takes it on his chin;
'The Perfesser' cantos in
sensing **Terminal Moraine**

and **The Dust** for 'The Messer'.
But no **Icarus Schmicarus**
The Apeman Cometh back
with a neat hexameter

into the solar plexus
of the Oxford Professor.
Critic, columnist, traveller ....
folds like a thesaurus;

A Vacant Possession
sign goes up in his eyes;
'that's for **Dumb Insolence'** cries
the champion of **Stufferation**.

A gasp is heard from Granta
'What's up with Auden's Heir?"
While down in Adrian's lair
the cheer is **Celia! Celia!**

Borrowing from **God, A Poem:**
'I won't be around for Salvation'
James 'The Perfesser' Fenton
parodies his **German Requiem**.

'Messer' Mitchell is terse
as Fenton falls flat:
'Sorry Bout That
but it could be verse!'

(Reference key to the publications and poems of the contenders: James Fenton – Terminal Moraine; A Vacant Possession; A German Requiem; The Kingfisher's Boxing Gloves and God, A Poem.

Adrian Mitchell – Out Loud; The Oxford Hysteria of English Poetry; The Dust; The Apeman Cometh; Icarus Schmicarus; Dumb Insolence; Stufferation; Celia Celia and Sorry Bout That).

Suck!

Tree sucks juice of earth - flower!
Bee sucks nectar of flower - honey!
Man sucks honey of bee - power!
Womb sucks sap of man - baby!
Baby sucks milk of mother - stronger!
Stronger sucks blood of weak - disaster!

At the close of play
it all sucks!

And I said, “Oh that I had wings like a dove!
for then I would fly away, and be at rest.”

Psalm LV verse 6

Glossary

TITLE:

Parable: a narrative of events used to typify moral or spiritual relations.

Prophet: One who foretells events. Teacher or interpreter of God's will. A false prophet is a lying deceptive charlatan.

Pillock: A foolish person; a blockhead.

Clusters

An international Treaty to ban the use of cluster bombs in modern warfare was scuttled by a refusal to sign by the major manufacturing countries of cluster bombs.

Lost in Transition

James R. Logan was a 19th Century lawyer who devoted his life to the pursuit of justice and knowledge. He was a champion of the non-European communities and rose to prominence when he defended an Indian betel-nut grower's rights against the formidable East India Company. He was born in Scotland in 1819 and died in Penang, Malaysia in 1869.

V.K.Lingam is a Malaysian lawyer whose questionable dealing with the highest echelons of the judiciary sparked a Royal Commission of Inquiry.

Boson & Morons: God's Particles

Barisan and *Pakatan* are the two largest political coalitions in Malaysia.

If Only Our Prophets Were Women
SIS is an acronym for Sisters in Islam - an activist organisation committed to raising awareness and defending the rights of Muslim women in Malaysia.

Fast not Feasting
balik kampung : back to the village.

Siege Mentality
Bolehland: Can-do-land i.e. Malaysia

Handkerchiefs (& Psalm 3)
Mahmoud Darwish is the great Palestinian poet who died in 2009.

Still Beautiful
Sir Bobby refers to Bobby Charlton,
the legendary English footballer; not to Sir Bobby Moore or Sir Bobby Robson!

Hibiscus
Cik is the Malay equivalent for *Miss*

Why Don't They Treat Old Men With Reverence?
Sadhu : an Indian wise man
Goondu: a stupid or foolish person
hum-sup: Chinese expression meaning 'lecherous'

Perils of the Native Tongue
Basmati: a type of fragrant rice

The Poet

This is Cecil Rajendra's 20th collection of poetry and marks over 40 years of creative writing.

His first collection - Embryo - was published in London in 1965 while still a student reading law at Lincoln's Inn.

His poems have been published in over 50 countries and been translated into several languages including German, French, Japanese, Malay, Tamil, Tagalog and Swahili.

On his return from London, Rajendra initiated Malaysia's first rural legal aid centre in a remote village offering pro-bono legal advice and assistance to farmers, fishermen and factory workers.

Rajendra is in private law practice and has served on the Malaysian Bar Council as Chairman of its Legal Aid and Human Rights Committees.

He is also a past President of the Human Rights Society of Malaysia (HAKAM).

In 2005, Cecil Rajendra was honoured as the first ever recipient of the Malaysia Lifetime Humanitarian Award for his pioneering legal aid work and inspirational poetry.

Previous Publications

1. Embryo (1965) - Regency Press (London & New York)
2. Eros & Ashes (1975) - Prakriti Press (London)
3. Bones & Feathers (1978) - Heinemann Educational Books (Asia) Ltd.
4. Refugees & Other Despairs (1980) - Choice Books Pte. Ltd. (Singapore)
5. Hour Of Assassins (1983) - Bogle-L'ouverture Publications (London)
6. Songs For The Unsung (1983) - WCC Publications (Geneva)
7. Postscripts (1984) - PMSB Publications (Malaysia)
8. Child Of The Sun (1986) - Bogle-L'ouverture Publications (London)
9. Dove On Fire (1987) - WCC Publications (Geneva)
10. Lovers Lunatics & Lallang (1989) - Bogle-L'ouverture Press (London)
11. Papa Moose's Nursery Rhymes (1991) - The Other India Press (Goa)
12. "25" (1991) - Practical Printers (Malaysia)
13. Zebrochene Traume (1992) - Horlemann (Germany)
14. Broken Buds (1994) - The Other India Press (Goa)
15. "31" (1997) - Prakriti Press (London)
16. Shrapnel Silence & Sand (1999) - Bogle-L'ouverture Press (London)
17. Rags & Ragas (2000) - Taraghale Publications (Nepal)
18. by Trial 'n Terror (2004) - Bogle-L'ouverture Press (London)
19. Tankas From A Tsunami (2006) - Bogle-L'ouverture Press (London)